THE ADVENTURES OF MR. FALLON FROULIE AND FRIENDS

Authored by Cassandra M. Allen

Illustrations by Christopher Martin

Published by Lee's Press and Publishing Company
www.LeesPress.net

This document is published by Lee's Press and Publishing Company located in the United States of America. It is protected by the United States Copyright Act, all applicable state laws and international copyright laws. The information in this document is accurate to the best of the ability of Cassandra M. Allen at the time of writing. The content of this document is subject to change without notice. This document is based on a nonfiction story with explicit urban language and slain.

ISBN-13: **978-0997862386** *Paperback*
ISBN-10: **0997862386**

This book is dedicated to my two greatest inspirations: Kobe & Michael Jr.

"I pray that your learning experiences be adventurous and fulfilling as mines"

Sincerely,

With all my love

Mom

Thank you Lord for giving me the gift to write and to reach children of the world showing them the true meaning of friendships, teamwork and patience through my books. In addition, for showing me that there is happiness after calamities and love after pain.

Once upon a time, there was a friendly farmer by the name of Mr. Fallon Froulie. He lived in a cabin on a farm with his animal friends in a little city known as Peppersville. Mr. Froulie, Cammi the bear, Penny the rabbit, Mimi the pig, Lillo and Louie the monkeys joined together and formed adventures, showed the meaning of friendships and learned how to work together.

Mr. Froulie awakes in the early morning and got out of bed. When Mr. Froulie puts on his overalls and heads out of his cabin, here comes along Cammi. Good morning, Mr. Froulie! Says Cammi. Good morning Cammi! Says Mr. Froulie. Then Cammi asks, are we going to go fishing and camping with Penny, Mimi, Lillo and Louie today? Sure, we are Cammi, but I have to go into town to the supermarket first! Mr. Froulie told Cammi. Ok sure, Cammi replies.

And then Mr. Foulie says, now you run along, I will see when I get back. Cammi starts walking back into the forest and Mr. Froulie grabs his carts of milk, his baskets of fruits and vegetables and puts them in his truck. He got into his truck and drove up the hill, heading towards town.

When Mr. Froulie finally arrived in town he took all the milk, fruits and vegetables out of his truck and sold them to Mr. Delyn at the supermarket. When Mr. Froulie left the supermarket, he walks around and says hello to all his friends in town but he runs into Mrs. Delyn. He had a big choice to make, Mrs. Delyn asks Mr. Froulie, are you coming to join Mr. Delyn and I for dinner this evening?

Oh, I'm sorry Mrs. Delyn, I promised Cammi and the rest of the gang that I would go fishing and camping with them. I'm very sorry. Then Mrs. Delyn says, that's ok Mr. Froulie, maybe some other time. Ok, says Mr. Froulie, then he walks back to his truck and drives back to his farm.

When Mr. Froulie finally arrives back at the farm. Cammi, Penny, Mimi, Lillo and Louie saw him coming and they all started walking to the cabin to see him with their camping bags, buckets and fishing rods in their hands. "Ok you guys," says Mr. Froulie, let me get my things too. Mr. Froulie walks into his cabin and grabs his camping things. When they all started walking along the forest trail, they found a camping site to share, and all worked together as a team to set up their camp site.

After Mr. Froulie, Cammi, Penny, Mimi, Lillo and Louie were all finished, they walked together in a line to go fishing at the lake. After Mr. Froulie, Cammi, Penny, Mimi, Lillo and Louie caught all the fish, they went back to their camp site. Before the sun started to set, they all worked together as a team once again and made the fire, so they could cook their fish for dinner.

After they all ate, sang songs, danced around the camp fire and told stories; the sun started setting. They finally fell asleep by the fire with their sweet dreams of more adventures to come.

The Illustrator

Chris Martin is an artist who is a North Carolina native. He attended North Carolina A&T State University where he graduated with a degree in visual arts and design. His passion is art and life wellness. He is currently a freelance professional while he is also starting his own alternative of health and coaching business.

THE END